How to Make
Something
from
Nothing

How to Make Something from Nothing

By **Rubye Mae Griffith**
and **Frank B. Griffith**

Photographs by **Bill Abrahams**

CASTLE BOOKS, NEW YORK

To the nothings—with the courage
to turn into somethings.

knowledgment

The authors acknowledge with sincere gratitude the help offered by those friends, neighbors, passers-by, and well-wishers who made an immeasurable contribution to this book by offering suggestions, advice, physical aid where necessary, and an endless, creatively stimulating supply of truly inspiring nothings.

Contents

How to Make
Something
from
Nothing

Getting Hooked

(A Chat With The Authors)

The majority of books you meet today have a noble purpose. We're speaking now of books with sufficient appeal for you to want to borrow them from a friend's library.

Such books usually tell their readers how to do something; how to be something; how to acquire something or how to become something.

We wish we could say the purpose of this book is noble but we must admit right now that it isn't. The only purpose of this book is to provide you with a lifelong addiction.

Read this book and you will never be the same.

You'll be obsessed with an insatiable, irresistible, inescapable desire *To Make Something from Nothing.*

And we guarantee that you will find within the pages of this book a way to satisfy your mad desire, as long as you make absolutely certain that the something you make from nothing has no relationship whatsoever to the original something for which the nothing was intended.

Observe this rule and it won't make a particle of difference how old you are; or how young you are; or how skilled you are; or how butter-thumbed . . . you'll not only be able to make something from nothing, you'll soon discover that it is possible to make something from *anything!*

All it takes is a wag's wit, a devil-may-care defiance of other people's opinions and a driving determination to bring a new, all-absorbing interest into your life.

Once you make something from nothing, you look at the world with new eyes. Wherever you go, whatever you see takes on new wonder, freshness and glamor. Because you see everything, not as it is, but as it will be *when you get through with it.*

Now don't say you're not creative enough to make something from nothing. You are!

We know. Because the minute we tell people the fun principle of making something from nothing, they not only want to make something right away, they come up with all sorts of helpful suggestions.

We received so many wonderful suggestions this way, from friends, neighbors and storekeepers, that we've included their contributions in this book—with their permission, of course—and with the understanding that each contributor will receive credit for his original idea.

So you see, you too can make something from nothing.

Just throw caution overboard.

Let yourself go.

And dare!

Having worked yourself into this state of fey and feckless frenzy you're ready to head for the city dump, the nearest junk yard, a local swap meet, garage sale, flea market, builder's emporium, or the super-drugstore—you name the destination.

It doesn't matter where you go or what you bring home as long as you see, in your mind's eye, the something to be made from your nothing.

This will be the turning point in your life.

This is known as "Getting Hooked." And there'll be no stopping you from then on.

That was exactly the way it happened to us.

We turned one nothing into something and we haven't stopped since. And we never intend to stop. Because making something from nothing, we've discovered, is more fun than any hobby you could name.

And besides the fun of digging out nothings and turning them into somethings, there's the additional fun of uncovering and discovering all sorts of hidden abilities you never knew you had.

You soon learn that when a particular skill is needed—such as soldering or mitring or planing or gouging or weaving or sanding or painting or planting or sketching or buffing or designing or digging—you develop that skill.

And you become *so frugal!*

Even if you were the world's biggest spender, suddenly you become frenetically frugal. Because you can't bear to throw away anything! And we mean *anything!*

Who knows when a toilet float may turn into an inkstand or some broken bits of glass may become a mosaic?

Old milk bottle tops, discarded gym socks, even chicken feathers, are fraught with all sorts of hidden potentials. They may turn into mobiles, mukluks, tiaras —they may turn into *anything!*

And here are some bonus boosters that you pick up along the way.

If you have young children you find dozens of ways to keep them happily occupied and out of mischief by teaching them how to make something from nothing—of course at the level of their skills.

Gold Fish Au Jewels.
(See page 56.)

Ivory Liquid Lady.
(See page 49).

Loop-the-Loop Golden Carafe.
(See page 51.)

Wild and Wonderful Wall Hanging.
(See page 43.)

Dog Food Box Lingerie Hamper.
(See page 26.)

Tillie the Tuna Tyke String Holder.
(See page 38.)

Paper Box Curler Caddy
(See page 76.)

Oatmeal Razzle Dazzle.
(See page 49.)

And, if you're a teacher, you come up with all sorts of thrilling new class projects. And the projects prove doubly delightful because the children bring their own nothings and you show them how to transform them into somethings —that's economical; and imagination is stimulated because the youngsters learn to be inventive.

On the other hand, if you're a teenager you soon realize that learning to make something from nothing really puts you out in front, because you're soon able to make your own jewelry, room decorations and gifts for your friends. And some things that you make are so wild you become the one who sets the fads for your group. And you're never bored because you're too busy creating.

If you're a young married, you and your husband can both get hooked. (When men get inventive in this fun game they make history!)

Pretty soon you find you're making conversation pieces that astound your friends. And some of your creations turn into family heirlooms that become the antiques of tomorrow.

Of course some projects can include the whole family and when this happens dad's workshop becomes the most popular hangout in the house.

Next you'll find your women's club making something from nothing. Then there'll be a race to see who makes the most unusual or distinctive something, and this competition adds a littly zesty challenge to the sport.

Senior Citizens also like making something from nothing. It solves their gift-giving problem for one thing, and for another, they find they don't have too much unused time on their hands.

Also, group therapists who work with the handicapped or the underprivileged say that teaching others to make something from nothing is not only enjoyable; it's therapeutic.

So wherever you find yourself, whatever your background or occupation, get busy today and start scrounging for "nothings" to make into "somethings."

Scrounging is the biggest part of the fun.

It takes you to new places where you meet new people and make new friends and it opens up a whole new world of stimulating ideas.

So now that we've warned you that you're starting on an addiction that you'll never be able to break we say: Cut loose! Have fun! Go forth this very minute and search for that mysterious, minute or marvelous nothing that you, and you alone, can turn into a scintillating, soul-shaking, heart stabbing *something!*

As you start on your high and heady adventure you'll enjoy the devilish, delirious, delightful and indescribable pleasure of *getting hooked.*

AND AWAY YE GO!

RENAISSANCE JACK

rounging through the yard of an abandoned home we came upon this jack crew, originally used to lift buildings and other heavy weights. We dusted it off and glued marbles in the holes where the turning rod would ordinarily be inserted and stuck an ancient red candle in the top.

The result is a massive and attractive patio candle that only the strongest may lift.

CRAFTY, THE KRAFT MUSTARD CLOWN

The minute we spied this Kraft Mustard Squeeze Bottle on our supermarket shelf we knew he'd make an adorable clown, and he did.

We couldn't wait to use up the mustard inside. And as soon as the plastic yellow bottle was empty we ran pipe cleaners through it for arms and covered them with bright red tissue paper. Then we painted a cupcake holder deep purple to make Crafty's collar. And we used a pinch of fiber glass shreds for his hair. (We lifted these from our son who uses them to patch his surfboard.)

We set Crafty's original top astride his hair for a hat, adding a blue pompom to it, then used beads and buttons for his eyes and nose and painted on black shoes.

Crafty is such a huge success as a party decoration, a nursery ornament or just to look at in the kitchen we've had to make a whole family of Craftys. (Good thing the family likes hot dogs and hot dogs can stand lots of mustard!)

19

DANCING DOLPHIN

If you don't happen to live on a ranch where the carcass of a cow may turn up in your stream bed, you may not be able to adorn your garden pool with a dancing dolphin of the type shown. This frivolous Flipper was made from the jawbone of a cow, bleached to mottled smoothness by long years of exposure to the sun. Surrounded by polished rocks found at the beach this flippant little fellow becomes an interesting attention-getter guaranteed to astonish your friends.

Our point in suggesting a dancing dolphin made from a cow's jaw, even though you personally may never meet up with a cow, is to encourage you to look for natural oddities native to your particular area. Who knows what you may find or what you may make of it. Anything goes when you aim to make something from nothing.

GIRAFFES GOSSIPING

These gossiping "Eves" were made, not from Adam's rib but from a cow's rib— three ribs to be exact. Anchored in modeling clay and surrounded by brush, they make an intriguing centerpiece for a children's party, or a permanent display in a boy's room.

INK STAND AND STATUETTE

Half the fun of making something from nothing is recalling where you found the original nothing and then chuckling over its ultimate transformation from a sow's ear into a silk purse.

The ink stand was originally a toilet float that had lain buried in a dump *for ten years,* thus acquiring a time-burnished patina of muted brown and puce tones. The stand itself was pulled from a pile of kindling and had just the right curvature in front to hold the quill pen which is really a guinea feather thrust in a round-end drawing pen. We painted a line around the stand, stuck a piece of cork atop the float and created a real conversation piece.

The lead statue legs were found in the yard of an abandoned home that once belonged to Laura La Plante, a movie star of the silent screen. Apparently it had once been an andiron, possibly the legs of a Revolutionary soldier. We stuck some feathers in it and it became a sort of winged Mercury. Next to it is the wood found inside those insulators you see atop telephone poles, weathered and beautiful and somehow atmospherically right for our headless soldier.

COOKIE PRESS KEY RINGS

Having trouble keeping old keys straight? We always did and always tried to open the garage with the house key and vice versa. Well now we just use our old cookie press cuttters for key charms and we never have trouble knowing which key is which. You can paint each design a different color or put initials or code symbols on them. In any event they're attractive and practical and everyone rushes out to make some just like them the minute they see ours.

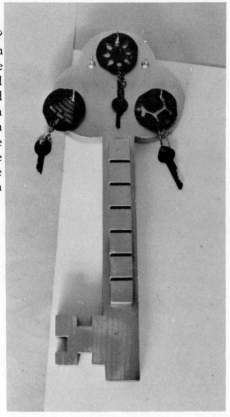

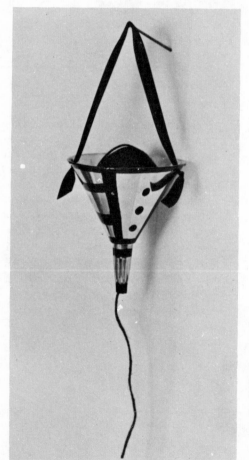

TIN FUNNEL YARN DISPENSER

This tin funnel had long outlived its usefulness as a means of pouring gasoline into our ranch gasoline can, but painted and hung aloft it became a yarn dispenser of great interest to Belinda, the ranch cat. You can also use a funnel dispenser for string, of course, in which case you'll want to hang it in workshop or kitchen.

FISH ON THE TABLE

Back a picture frame with plywood and anchor legs from an old coffee table to the frame. Paint frame and legs black. Fill frame with ready-mix cement or plaster of Paris and embed bits of broken colored glass in the mixture before it dries. Now you have a distinctive and colorful patio table. Other designs could be a simple flower, rooster, bird or cat.

THUNDERMUG TUREEN

Do you have an old thundermug that is standing around collecting dust? Startle your more sophisticated friends by using it for a soup tureen. Or, if you prefer, fill with artificial flowers and use as a centerpiece.

Suggestion contributed by
WANITA DRAPER

CANDLE, CANDLE, BURNING BRIGHT (?)

The brown ceramic candleholder is actually an insulator from a high power line. The candle is a fake made by sticking bits of green, blue and brown wax (melted down from crayons and old candles) to the tube from a package of kitchen foil.

Suggestion contributed by
VIVIENNE MOORE

HOME MADE BATH SALTS

To make your own bath salts at about one-tenth the market price add a tablespoon of glycerine and two teaspoons of food coloring of your choice to a five-pound package of Epsom Salts and perfume with about ten drops of the dregs from old perfume bottles. Now you have a water softener and body beautifier that adds glamor to your bathroom when displayed in an old vinegar bottle decorated with a foil-covered cork and a bit of ribbon.

INSULATOR BOOKENDS

The blue-green glass insulators you see atop telephone poles sometimes fall to the ground after wind storms and if you're lucky enough to find any still unbroken they make colorful bookends and paperweights.

DEER ANTLER SALAD TONGS

Does your husband go on a yearly hunting spree? If he does have him give you a pair of deer antlers; paint them white with black trim and use for salad tongs remembering this one caution: Use lead-free nonpoisonous paint and lead-free, waterproof varnish.

BEE SMOKER BELLOWS

Found in a junk shop one bee smoker, used by beekeepers to blow smoke into a hive when they want to "settle" the bees so as to be able to extract their honey without interference. Painted black with pink design and trim, the bee smoker makes an excellent bellows for your fireplace.

DOG FOOD BOX LINGERIE HAMPER

This beautiful lingerie hamper was once a humble dog food box. To make it we covered a twenty-pound size Walter Kendall Fives heavy cardboard dog food box with bright floral-patterned giftwrap paper in tones of pale yellow and lime green on the outside. Then we lined the inside with variegated Madras Tissue.

This tissue is striped in hot orange, vivid yellow and rich warm brown so that the overall effect is one of thrilling color.

The trimmings consist of green glass gem mosaics pasted in a border around the flap of paper that overhangs the box. And the leaf pattern on the lid is made of three large emerald mosaics with a green artificial flower leaf for a stem.

Walter Kendall Dog Food Boxes are so sturdy and strong and capacious that they also make excellent wastebaskets, yarn holders and toy chests.

STRING FLOWER WALL HANGING

Gild a piece of three-quarter-inch plywood 29 inches by 9 inches. Paste on floral design of green twine. Add green glass gem mosaics. Circle with green rubber bands. Form pods of pink and orange pop beads.

CURLER TREE IN BLOOM

The next best thing to a money tree is this amusing little curler tree. To make it we filled a styrofoam base—you could use any cardboard box or metal receptacle of suitable size—with plaster of Paris.

Just before the plaster dries insert four long thin pieces of doweling on which to thread the curlers. We painted the base light blue with black trim and pasted on pastel tile mosaics.

You could use red hots or looseleaf reinforcement rings painted various colors as trimming if you like.

Stand on your dressing table and you'll never have to paw in a drawer for your curlers again.

Contributed by
LILLIAN GREER

DAVY JONES'S LOCKET

Here's a way to convert an old refrigerator storage box of clear plastic into a charming nursery display piece.

Arrange a seascape inside the container of shells, artificial flower leaves, copper scouring pad curls and some of that shredded green waxed paper you find in Easter baskets.

Paint the outside with green seaweed squiggles, cover the front with clear cellophane and set a night light behind your finished masterpiece.

Just remember not to put the light bulb too close to the plastic.

ICE CREAM SPOON POP ART PAINTING

The background of this wild and wonderful pop art painting is a piece of unpainted plywood edged in black plastic tape. The design is formed by pasting ice cream spoons painted in five different bright colors to the plywood in a free form pattern. The result: "Footprints on the Sands of Time," a painting to brighten up nursery or rumpus room.

Contributed and executed by
MARTHA GRIFFITH

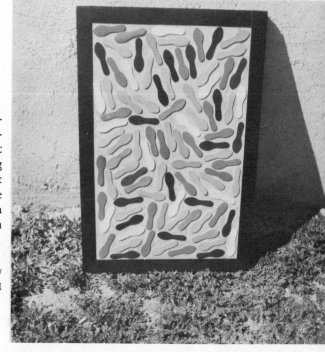

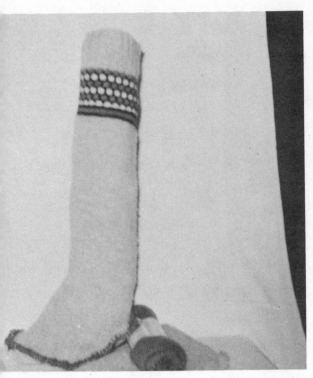

MUKLUK MADE FROM SWEATER SLEEVE

Is there a moth-eaten, outgrown sweater in the house? Remove the sleeves and feather stitch to a leather sole taken from an old slipper or cut from any leather scrap. Now you have a pair of warm, snug mukluks for home lounging.

"MOD MAID'S" CURLER COVER-UP

This "Op" Top made from a piece of mattress ticking is edged with black ruffling and white eyelet to become a fetching bonnet that you can wear with aplomb to the supermarket. The sewn-in earrings are made from curtain rings.

SHOE SHINE KIT HOUSEHOLD CADDY

A neglected shoe shine kit, painted white and trimmed with snips of black plastic tape, becomes a handy household caddy in which to tote cleaning aids from parlor to bedroom to sink.

ABALONE SHELL GROTTO

Paste a picture from a Sunday School magazine inside an abalone shell and place an artificial Lily of the Valley in the bottom; then make a bracket of two pieces of wood nailed together and covered with a gold paper doily and you have a delightful hanging or standing miniature shrine.

BIRD IN A GILDED CAGE

To make this graceful, delicate bird cage, gild twenty-four coat hangers and tape together at the center, handles out, hooks pointing upward. Slip brass link plumber's chain over hooks and fasten a loop of the same chain through hangers at the top and bottom of the cage, drawing tightly. Now remove the taping from the coat hangers and fill the cage. We used two plastic fern fronds, a paper bird, glass beads and pop beads to crown the hooks of the hangers—all in shades of wild pink and violet orange and singing yellow.

Suggestion contributed by
BEA BENTON

31

BIRD CAGE STAND PICTURE FRAME

Has the bird flown its nest? Then use the stand from its former home as a unique picture frame. Decorate the stand with artificial flowers, leaves or berries and hang the picture in the center, using a ribbon or a chain.

The "painting" seen here consists of a piece of plywood on which we pasted a picture cut from the descriptive booklet of the world famous Lippizaner Riding School of Vienna. We shellacked over the picture and pasted plastic tape around the edges to form a pseudo-frame.

MODERNISTIC SPOOL BOUQUET

Save your old sewing spools—cardboard or wooden ones—paint them in bright geometric patterns and cover one end with masking tape. Now stain slender dowels or the stems from balloons a leaf green and slide a spool on one end. The vase we used was made from a drain spout painted white with black tear drop spots; the bottom was taped with black plastic tape.

Suggestion contributed by
Vivienne Moore

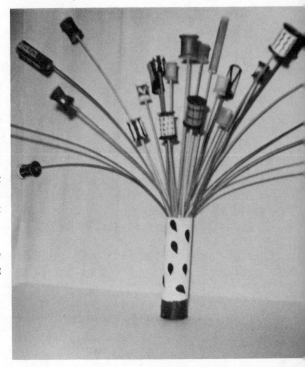

STIRRUP ASH TRAY

This stirrup from a very old side saddle was made into an ash tray simply by gluing a small white dish to the bottom.

BIRD ON NEST TABLE

The top of this coffee table was made from an old piece of board weathered to a soft beige by years of sun and rain. We attached it to the legs from an old couch, painted the edges and the legs black, and splattered and dripped on the design, using thick paint and blobs of sealing wax.

GOLD JEWELED CHEST

A friend of ours found this well-made nicely lined, hinged box discarded outside an electronics parts plant where it had been used as a receptacle in which to ship delicate instruments. We gilded it, added rick rack and glass gem mosaics and it became our personal jewel case.

Suggestion contributed by
ROBERT BANE

COFFEE POT CATCH-ALL

The coffee pot, a white agate one, was found in the ground when we were gardening and, surprisingly enough, had only one chip but lots of rust. We cleaned it up, painted inside and trim with forest green Pactra enamel and added a bouquet of violets. Standing near the stove it makes an excellent catch-all for your kitchen spoons. Or, if you wish to use it as an ornament, paint old spoons in vivid shades of pink, green and yellow and stand on your kitchen window sill.

KITCHENWARE PLANTER

brass planter sans brass—having spent
ars in a dump—was reclaimed to make
is very "now" planter. We painted it
ack and filled it almost to brim with
aster of Paris in which we stuck a
okie press plunger, a coffee percolator
em topped with the head from an egg
ater, a fish skinner grasping a spring—
upside down. Next we wound in curls
om heavy foil and the result is a glitter-
g modern display piece. We poured
ushed windshield glass on top of the
aster of Paris to add sparkle. Pretty
nsational and liked by all who see it.

HOMEMADE KNITTING NEEDLES

Short of steel knitting needles? Have
your husband cut you a set from coat
hangers. After cutting to size all he has
to do is grind the ends to points and
polish to smoothness.

Suggestion contributed by
WANITA DRAPER (*but Andy Draper
made them.*)

SCRAP-MADE POT HOLDERS

Photo shows pot holders made from scraps of chintz filled with squares cut from old mattress covers. Old table pads may also be used and almost any upholstery, drapery or carpet swatch may be used in a pinch.

Suggestion contributed by
WANITA DRAPER

BUTTERFLY WALL PLAQUE

This really beautiful little wall plaque is made from a thin plywood scrap 6 inches by 4½ inches. We painted it sage green with Pactra enamel then bordered it with Eucalyptus pods painted orange, pink and red. (You could use beans or shells if you like.) The body of the butterfly is made from two plastic caps taken from Duragloss Lipstick cards in Tangerine color. We added yellow wings made from rubber bands and three pink and yellow pop beads. Antennae are rubber bands.

HUB CANDLE HOLDER

Years spent underground in our iron-rich western soil turned this wagon wheel hub a beautiful antiqued rusty hue, very Etruscan looking. Some accident squashed the hub, giving it a wonderfully unique appearance. All we did was trim with the mosaics to make a magnificent sturdy patio candle holder. And the candle, though shielded from drafts, provides a rich golden glow through the hub interstices.

SKIPPING LAMB PLAQUE

What happier way for a youngster to count sheep than with this amusing wall hanging made from a three-quarter-inch plywood scrap 13½″ long by 7½″ high. The lamb is made from a shocking pink and orange yarn tassel. The butterfly is lime green and turquoise felt with red antennae. The lamb's tail is magenta felt and the rickrack is orange and purple, the toothpicks green and blue. And the background is sunniest yellow.

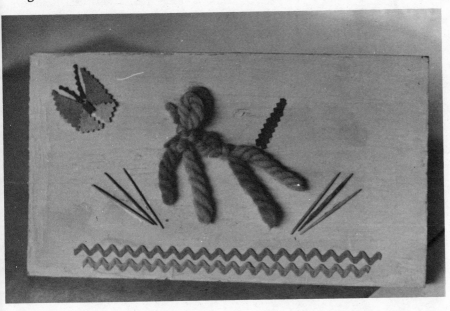

PLASTIC HOSIERY HAMPER

Plastic slipper case was painted with red Pactra enamel and then we covered flap with glue and traced glue flower pattern on front. We sprinkled gold glitter on the glued areas and when dry taped the case to a child's hanger painted black. Hung in the closet or bathroom it makes a handy hosiery hamper.

TILLIE THE TUNA TYKE STRING HOLDER

Tillie is made from a tuna can. Remove one end and cover the other with muslin and then a layer of clear plastic or Saran Wrap, anchoring to the can with a sturdy rubber band. Face is made from buttons, felt and yarn scraps. Hat is made from flowered gingham bordered in rickrack The hat has a draw string in back so you can open it and insert a ball of string or yarn. Tillie carries her scissors behind her left ear, hooked through a curtain ring. She smiles up the whole kitchen when you hang her on the wall.

Contributed and executed by
CELIA HODENKAMP

FIRST LADY TRAY

To make this attractive serving tray or
wall ornament we painted the top of a
10-inch fruit cake tin muted orange and
pasted on a First Lady decked in white,
cut from an American Heritage Magazine,
then added bright yellow lilies. Sprayed
with varnish the end result is not only
beautiful, it smacks very definitely of the
antique.

DRAMATIC EAR LOOPS FROM BLACK CURTAIN HOOPS

These sensational earrings were made by
fastening black plastic curtain rings measuring two inches in diameter to ear-bobs.
It's as simple as that.

SPIN THE GILDED BOTTLE

Want a wonderful new spin the bottle game to play at parties and showers? Just paste every conceivable object that you can find to a bottle, then gild the whole thing. This bottle is decorated with toothpaste tubes, fountain pens, springs, buttons, razor blades, combs, jewelry, hardware, and about 150 more items. You allow your guests to study it for thirty seconds, whisk it away and ask them to write down the things they remember seeing on it. The one who remembers the most takes first prize. Makes a wonderful hostess gift.

Suggestion contributed and executed
by WANITA DRAPER

LITTLE DOVES IN A YARN TREE

The breathtakingly beautiful color of this nursery plaque must be seen in order for you to appreciate its sensational impact. It is made from an old bread board 11¼ inches wide by 19 inches long painted clear bright lemon yellow. The grass is kelly green yarn. The tree trunk is shocking pink cording. The birds are cut from bright blue, green, purple and red tissue paper. Flowers, made from coils of yarn, are turquoise blue, purple and olive green. Everyone who sees this little wall hanging falls in love with it for it sings a song of vibrant color that reaches straight to the heart.

INDIAN CANDLE FROM LEFTOVERS

Save your leftover candle ends, remove the wicks, and when you have a fairly large collection, melt them down in a foil pie pan and pour them in a milk carton, suspending a piece of string from a pencil over the carton to form a new wick. Before your eyes a new candle will grow.

Sometimes the color won't be too brilliant, as happened in the case of the candle shown here, so to enliven it we pasted on bits of bright yellow, orange and brown tissue paper cut in Indian motifs. We added a few pop beads, sticking them on with small sequin pins, then a touch of orange rickrack.

The secret of making Indian motifs from tissue paper is to cut the paper in squares or rectangles, fold in half, then cut away with your manicuring scissors, turning the paper this way and that with carefree abandon. When you open the paper you'll have a Rorschach personality indicator or an Indian design, depending on your point of view.

DRAGUETTES IN FLOWER

Draguettes, those multi-color tiny round cookie decorations that come in delicate pastel shades as well as gold and silver, make a sweet ornament for a child's room if you paste them, as we did, on a six by six wood scrap painted forest green. The flower pot is a shell covered with gold foil. So simple to make even a very young child can do it with little supervision; but the result is ethereal and lovely.

41

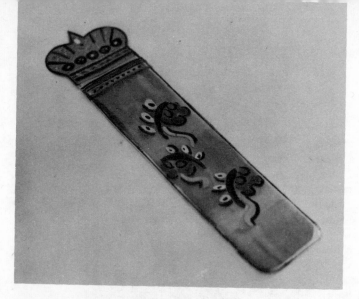

KING-SIZE BOOKMARK

This striking, regal, washable bookmark is made from the plastic case in which a hairband once reposed. We slipped a piece of brilliant pink and red varigated Madras Tissue paper inside and painted the outside with Pactra enamel in brilliant shades of purple, blue, red and turquoise. The top was gold to start with. Since the plastic case measures 11½ inches by 2¾ inches, you really have a king-size bookmark for weighty tomes.

OVEN ROASTER CANDLE SCONCE

Have a welder cut a slit in the bottom of the lower part of an old oven roaster and punch a hole about a third of the way down the back so you can hang it up. Paint the oven roaster black. Insert a piece of tin cut from the top of a coffee can in the slit you had made. The tin can cover provides a support for a candle which you stand on it. We placed the candle in the collar from a faucet turned upside down. Now paint a background design in glue and sprinkle with gold glitter and you have a handsome candle sconce to hang on patio wall or tree. The top of the roaster makes a matching sconce treated the same way.

WILD AND WONDERFUL
WALL HANGING

While junk scrounging one day we came upon one of those pieces of circular tin that you hang over a hole in the wall when you remove a stove pipe.

What to do with it?

The answer came when we painted our stove pipe cover-up throbbing orange, pulsating purple and shocking pink and pasted it to a square of raffia that we painted a wild tangerine.

The resulting wall hanging is really a thriller—not for timid souls—but a riot of shrieking color for those brave enough to live with it.

HIDEAWAY FOR CROCHET HOOKS

Have you often wished you had a safe and special place in which to store your crochet hooks? Well, just take a Kraft Grated Parmesan Cheese dispenser, decorate it any way you like and slip the crochet hooks inside. We painted ours a delicate french blue trimmed in purple and pasted on a lace paper doily also painted purple. Very chic, and very handy.

Suggestion contributed by
LILLIAN GREER

CLEANSER CAN FLOWER HOLDER

This white plastic Dutch Cleanser container made a refreshing kitchen flower holder when we painted the top and bottom half forest green and pasted a strip of pale green satin ribbon around the middle. All we had to do was insert small artificial roses in the holes in the top!

The same kind of cleanser cans cut in half make excellent bathroom glasses or picnic glasses.

BATHTUB FLOTILLA

This trim, spanking bathtub flotilla for the younger set is made from old bath sponges and worn out scraps from Pioneer Bluettes rubber gloves.

Just string the sponges together by running plastic beads through them (you can push them right through) and run a piece of stiff wire down through each sponge at the front end, bending it at the bottom to hold it in place and tilting it backward slightly to give a smart pitch to the sail.

Now cut six small triangles from old rubber gloves and paste them together on either side of the wires. The fleet is now ready to sail.

UPSIDE DOWN FLOWER HOLDER

This lovely creation, while sinfully simple to make, proves a cloche needn't be gauche. To make it we turned a beige, buckram-lined wool cloche hat upside down and fastened a strip of turquoise plastic webbing from an outdoor lounge chair around the middle with a paper fastener. We added another strip of the same turquoise webbing for a handle, fastening it with two more paper fasteners and piled in artificial lilacs.

The lavender, beige and turquoise color scheme just blends beautifully and the "planter" may be stood on a table or hung from a bird cage hook.

PANTS-WORK QUILT

If you have enough men (who wear pants) in your life, sufficient patience and the right amount of skill, you too can make a Pants-Work Quilt like the one shown here. Then, as your reward, you will own a handsome, distinctive lap warmer, guaranteed to last and last and last because it is made entirely of wool and worsted.

Contributed and executed
by WANITA DRAPER

KNIT KIT FOR KNIT WITS

This is not a telescope, though it may resemble one, it's a kit for those who knit. Made from an aluminum foil inner cardboard, it will hold a whole flock of short, medium and long knitting needles —and you can hang them up out of the reach of kinder and pets. We gilded the foil tube and pasted on chinese red yarn interspersed with pearls. But you could cover yours in black vinyl and paint a gold or white knitting needle on the front, or decorate with knitting abbreviations.

The big question, of course, was how to find something that would just fit in the ends, and here we were lucky. We took the end from one of those foil rollers that has little white plastic knobs on the end to make it self-dispensing—and the knob just fit. We painted it red and pasted on a button covered with gold foil to take care of the top.

Then we found that an old plastic stamp dispenser, the kind you put a roll of stamps in, just fit the bottom, and tight enough to hold without further help. We punched holes for the cord handle and knotted the cord inside and the whole problem was solved.

Suggestion contributed by
LILLIAN GREER

STYROFOAM GIFT WRAP

In the accompanying pictures you see a gift wrap that also makes a gift. It is made from the packing from an electric toothbrush and it may be that you won't meet up with one exactly like it. But most of us do come across styrofoam packings from various small appliances, and we include the directions for making this unique gift just in case it may inspire you to do something similar but not identical.

We painted the packing to resemble a nursery block and put a handle on it that would still permit it to open as it was meant to. With a child's gift placed inside it you can present it at a nursery shower and win wild acclaim because chances are no one else will bring along a gift in a wrapping as practical as the gift itself.

This same principle of placing a gift inside an amusing, reuseable gift wrap can be applied to other kinds of showers with all sorts of happy results.

We used tempera paint and plastic tape for our decorations but you may find it simpler to just paste on cut-outs from old children's books or current magazines.

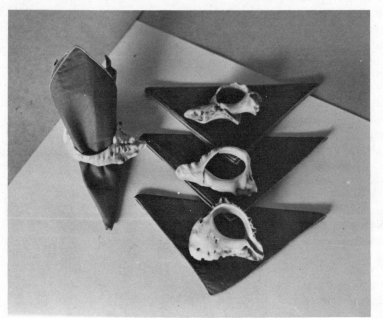

SHELL NAPKIN RINGS

Our friend, Ginny Clausen, tells us that these beautiful, creamy-white shells are from left-handed whelk—you'll note that their swirls all run to the left—and she swears there are right-handed whelk, though she never met any.

We looked up "whelk" in our Webster's and found that a whelk is a "gastropod" now obsolete. This may mean that you won't be able to find any where you live, but whether you do or not, you may find some shells that will make pretty and practical napkin rings; and if you don't, try using discarded plastic or papier mâché bracelets for your napkins, they work just as well.

Creative spark supplied by
GINNY CLAUSEN

GET AHEAD OR PUT A HEAD ON YOUR SAVINGS

In the interests of beautifying America we realized that someone should find an aesthetic use for discarded beer cans, so we created this beer can bank. Just paint the beer can (we did ours in black); then paste on Gay Nineties prints culled from old magazines. We found ours from old American Heritage Magazines. This one of the two stovepipe gentlemen is typical. Many are hilarious and show maidens swooning and others being saved from a fate worse than death.

If you prefer, of course, you can make your bank from juice cans. The bigger the can the bigger the deposit, eventually. Tin can banks make wonderful club or group projects, you can make them so quickly and inexpensively and it's so much fun.

Suggestion contributed by
CELIA HODENKAMP

OATMEAL RAZZLE DAZZLE

One of the most spectacular and at the same time practical somethings we've ever made from nothing is this glittering Razzle Dazzle Patio Whirler that you hang out to keep the birds away from your fruit trees or just to amaze and confound your guests.

To make it we covered a large Quaker Oats Box with kitchen foil, taped the ends with black three-quarter-inch plastic tape, and secured a handle of heavy cord by knotting it through the top. Then we pasted on bits of broken glass in bright reds, blues, greens and browns and added fragments of mirror. We bordered the mirrored pieces with black plastic tape to enhance the design.

Because of the way the handle is attached the Razzle Dazzle whirls constantly, first in one direction, then in the other, and as the sunlight hits the mirrors it throws off flashing light patterns reminiscent of Lawrence Welk and the Palladium Ballroom.

Makes a wonderful housewarming gift!

IVORY LIQUID LADY

Don't ever throw away your liquid detergent bottles. Here's an example of the lovely party and shower decorations you can make with them. The Ivory Liquid bottle (this is the pint size) has a natural yoke collar that only requires painting to make the start of a beautiful dress. We placed a cork in the top of the bottle, covered it with cotton and pasted on hair of copper scouring curls, sequin eyes, plastic tape lashes and a sequin cut in half for the mouth.

We painted the bottle French Blue and lavender and added purple rickrack and sequins. The arms are made by pushing a wire or pipe cleaner through the bottle and covering with strips of pale blue Kleenex tissues. The hands and halo are the gold foil tops from Girard Salad Dressing Bottles and the wings are cut from a T.V. dinner tray and gilded, then pasted to the back of the bottle.

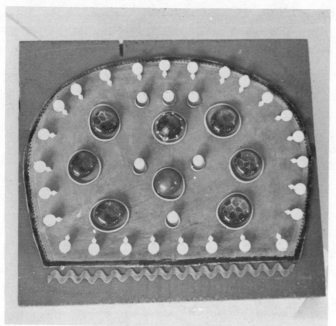

CROWN LEATHER WALL PLAQUE

We're almost ashamed to tell you how we made this elegant appearing, colorful wall plaque for our den, but then we told you anything goes when you start to make something from nothing. The background is a wood scrap 10½ by 10 inches painted vivid kelly green. The leather crown is the former knee guard from a pair of discarded riding breeches. We pasted on a border of white pop beads and a few additional pop beads in wild pink and brash orange. Then we scattered some green glass gem mosaics here and there and circled them with turquoise rubber bands and put a strip of lime green rickrack across the bottom.

MACARONI NECKLACES

We snitched some of our La Rosa Macaroni from the pantry to make these fashionable, bright colored necklaces. The top one is made from La Rosa Rigatoni #27 painted with Kelly Green Tempera and tied with navy blue and lime green yarn.

The lower necklace is made from La Rosa Salad Macaroni, two strands painted vivid yellow, two painted brilliant orange. Both are strung on old fishing line.

LOOP-THE-LOOP GOLDEN CARAFE

Spray a discarded distilled water bottle with gold paint and add pink, yellow, orange and raspberry flavored Fruit Loops, the kids' favorite breakfast cereal; trail on some olive green yarn, and you too can amaze your friends with this glorious golden carafe, guaranteed to stimulate conversation at a glance.

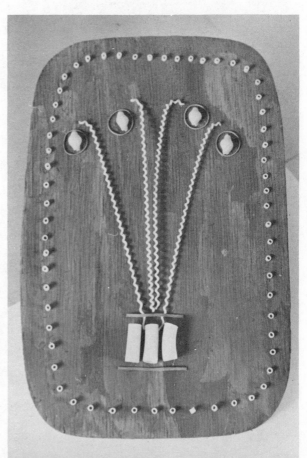

MACARONI PLANT PLAQUE

The background of this delicate and arresting wall hanging is the top of an old wooden picnic basket 11 inches by 16 inches painted a rose-red with Tempera.

The border is made from La Rosa Salad Macaroni, the base from La Rosa Rigatoni #27, the stems from La Rosa Slip Pruf Spaghetti #115 (no kidding); and the flowers from La Rosa Macaroni Shells #22. The lines above and below the base are bright green rubber bands.

Go thou and do likewise and you'll have a good chuckle provoker for a children's room that is also very aesthetic.

NIGHT STAND ASHTRAY AND NIGHT LIGHT

Graceful, dainty and practical. And you'd never believe this lovely bedside ornament started out as a plain steel bookend. We painted it white, added nine shells painted inside with pale pink nail polish and attached another larger shell to be used as an ashtray. Next we tucked green plastic leaves here and there and some lily of the valley and a few lilac flowerets. Set a little night light a few inches behind the bookend and you have a charming night light and also a most welcome gift.

ALL IS NOT GOLD THAT GLITTERS

If you have the patience to paste macaroni bows and shells all over an old toilet seat and then gild with gold spray paint, you too can become the proud owner of this astonishing portrait frame.

One caution: We do not recommend that you use it to frame your rich Uncle John's picture!

Suggestion contributed by
WANITA DRAPER

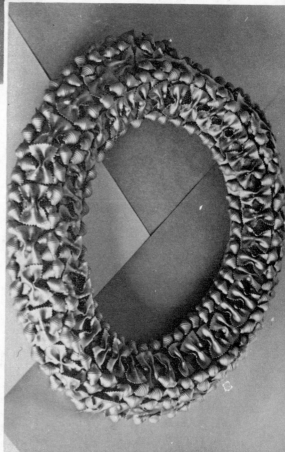

A ROSE IS A ROSE—OR IS IT?

Made from a brilliant orange yarn scrap this lifelike rose has a green straw for a stem and olive green yarn swirls for leaves. It is pasted to a sheet of sun yellow construction paper mounted on a piece of cardboard 17 inches by 14 inches. The center sheet is edged in pink and bright green. The cardboard border is painted shocking pink and the scrollwork is bright green. The riot of color blooms year round and fairly vibrates with cheerfulness.

KINGDOM OF THE SEA
SHADOW BOX

This ancient picture frame, painted white and backed with cardboard, became a shadow box to which we added two shelves of thin board supported by short pieces of doweling. Sea shells displayed in the shadow box hold bits of leaves from discarded artificial flowers. The "fish" rising to the surface are burned out camera flashbulbs, the blue ones. The interior of the frame and shelves are painted a matching blue.

CHRISTMAS BULB PLANT

Fill an old flower pot with plaster of Paris or pebbles and run a stiff wire down through the center, anchoring it at the bottom and allowing it to rise about 15 inches above the pot. Paint pot turquoise and trim with black plastic tape. Wire old Christmas light bulbs to the main stem using straws with pipe cleaners run through them. Tape where the light bulb joins the stem with green florist tape. Add cupcake holders in pastel shades as frills for the light bulbs and you have a cheerful little plant that never needs watering.

If you prefer to use workable light bulbs you'll have to use stiff wire for the stems and tape the bulb wires to this with fireproof tape. Use silver or colored foil for your light frills instead of paper and place near lamp outlet so you can light at night. This makes a beautiful night light for a hallway. Be sure plaster of Paris is thoroughly dry before plugging in.

PINE CONE CIGARETTE DISPENSER

Most successful something ever to be made from a nothing! And so easy! Just spray paint a giant-size pine cone gold or your favorite color, slip cigarettes and tiny match boxes in place and you have one of the smartest and most practical cigarette dispensers ever to perk up a party.

GIGANTIC FUN FLOWER

Making a sunflower can be fun. Just take a circle of brown felt 20 inches in circumference, back with a cardboard disc the same size and paste on a circle of leaves about 6 inches long and 2½ inches wide.

The leaves are made by cutting a cardboard pattern for each leaf and pasting yellow drapery fabric to the front and back of each pattern. You'll want about twenty-two leaves.

With the leaves securely grounded you're ready to add a backing of another felt circle. Insert a dowel stick for a stem and cut leaves from a loop rug scrap (ours are blue and green in color) and slide them up the dowel stick.

Paste some deep blue and green glass gem mosaics on the front of your sunflower and now you have a spectacular ornament for den or rumpus room.

OUT OF THE DEPTHS—A MARVEL

Buried in a dump for ten years, the metal stand you see here pretending that it has always been a magazine rack, was once used to hold nuts and bolts in a hardware store. It was so rusty when we unearthed it we despaired of reclaiming it. But after soaking off the rust with kerosene and painting it glossy black we realized we had made a rare find. All we did was add turquoise plastic chair webbing and a strip of black rickrack and we had ourselves a handsome and capacious magazine rack.

GETTING DOWN TO NUTS AND BOLTS

One day we told a friend we could make something from anything and she pointed to a can of nuts and bolts we had standing by at the time and said, "Okay, make something from them."

We painted a thin scrap of plywood 6½ inches by 5½ inches French Blue and pasted on toggle bolts, fish sinkers and ball bearings—some painted black, some left their natural silver finish. Then we edged our nutty little plaque in black and gave it to our friend as an ornament for her son's room.

She had to admit it is possible to make something from (*almost*) anything!

GOLDFISH AU JEWELS

Alas, poor cutting board, we knew it well. Little did we know that bejeweled and bedazzled it would acquire sufficient bezaz to hang on our wall in shining splendor.

All we did was spray our fish board gold and add multi-color gem mosaics held on by sealing wax drippings. Then we dribbled black and gold sealing wax fore and aft to make a nose and tail and added two fins of brass grille wire. We held the fins in place by submerging a mosaic completely in gold sealing wax.

We painted part of the background bright turquoise and part pale gold to give a sun-splashed effect and drilled two holes by which to hang our finny fellow. Brass plumber's chain looped through the holes makes a good sturdy method of hanging because this cutting board is made from inch-thick plywood and it's pretty solid.

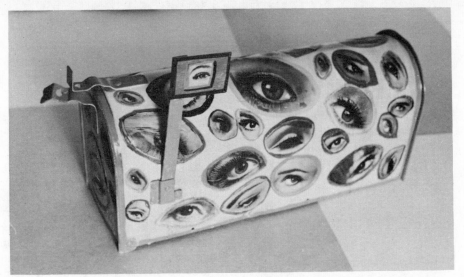

MAILBOX CARRY-ALL

Here's how a beat-up and battered old mailbox took a new lease on life.

We painted it white and covered it with glamorous, gorgeous feminine eyes cut from magazines and outlined the eye cut-outs in bright green, blue, purple, pink and lime; we trimmed the mailbox in shocking pink, then varnished the whole thing with clear varnish to make it weatherproof.

It made a perfect gift for a teenager to attach to her bike as a carry-all for lunch and books, and when she locks it she knows it's tamper-proof—especially with all those eyes standing guard over it.

ON THE RECORD

Have you always longed to have your own golden record collection? Now you can.

Just spray an old record with gold paint—you can get these old records at the Goodwill or Salvation Army for five cents or less—and add any dried weeds or seed pods you can find and spray them. Do one or a series; hang in record room, den or a teenager's room. You can do them in color if you wish.

Originally intended in their golden state as Christmas door ornaments, these records look too nice to take down after Christmas; you'll want to leave them on display all year.

Contributed by
JUNE PETERSEN

BIRD CAGE PLANTER

This wicker bird cage, cast on the scrap heap, once housed a papier mâché parrot, the star of a college play. We gilded it, filled it with flowers and hung it in our patio—and you can do likewise, if you find the right scrap heap.

A-TISKET A-TASKET, WHAT HAPPENED TO OUR BASKET?

This once-modest wicker cheese basket, gilded and encrusted with glittering masses of jewelry and shells, suddenly acquired a new and glamorous personality. Now it's easily the prettiest little basket on the beach and even looks sweet with summery swirling dance dresses.

CAUSE FOR REFLECTION

We seem to have a way of attracting old defective mirrors that have lost their sparkle as well as their frames. We never could decide what to do with them besides using them as a base for a miniature garden, but here's a treatment we stumbled on that really gives a dejected mirror new zip.

We painted on a frame of shocking pink and orange, then pasted strips of Madras Tissue Paper lengthwise down the front of the mirror in the same shocking pink, orange tones. Over these strips we pasted cut out upholstery flowers in vivid shades of burnt orange, purple and turquoise with bright emerald green leaves.

Our shocking pink and orange riotous mirror is so outspoken it usually elicits gasps from guests but we love it.

FROTHY FILLIP FOR SUNGLASSES

Remove the plastic top from last year's date pad, paint it pale blue or green and wire it to your sunglasses and look who has a smart sun visor!

ANGELIC WALL ORNAMENT

Wait! Don't throw away the foil container that frozen dinners come in. Paint
the edges black, fill with cement or plaster
of Paris and while the cement or plaster
is still moist embed bits of broken colored
glass in it.

Angels or flower patterns are easy to
make and the brilliance of the glass provides all the excitement needed to make
these little plaques colorful and interesting.

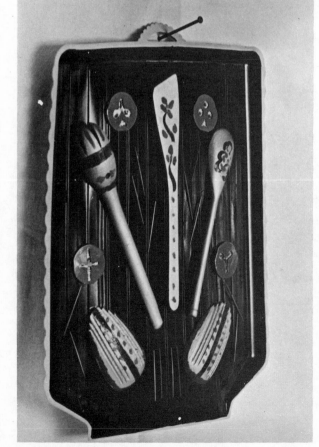

NO NEED TO BE BORED WITH
YOUR DRAINBOARD

Must old drainboards go down the
drain? This one almost did—several times.
Then we painted it black, edged it in
aqua, added gilded spoons trimmed with
bright green and pink designs and pasted
on cookie press cutters painted shocking
pink with gold foil centers. We added
blue and green plastic toothpicks and now
we have a beautiful wall ornament for
our pantry.

HOW TO MAKE DOUBLE
FROM NOTHING

Hang your head if you've been throwing out empty white plastic bleach bottles of the Clorox variety. Cut them in half and make a plant hanger out of the top half simply by running plastic lace through the top and looping the lace through a curtain ring. Cover the cap with black plastic tape.

Then spray the bottom half with gold paint, attach a brass drawer pull to the top for a handle and decorate with strips of ribbon smocking, rickrack, velvet ribbon or what-have-you and add a few glass gem mosaics for the luxury touch. Now you have a glittering dome to hide that spare roll of toilet tissue or anything else you may want to hide.

LITTLE CURLER CUTIE DOLL

Here's a perfect hanging toy for the crib set. Or it makes an amusing nursery ornament.

Just tie together three large, 2½ inch and two smaller 1¼ inch plastic hair curlers.

Tie four bright yarn pompoms to the ends of the curlers for hands and feet.

Add a fishing bob at the top for a head. The cap is already there; all you have to do is add the face.

Slip a keychain through the hook at the end of the fishing bob and it's ready for hanging.

We used a red, white and blue color scheme. You could paint yours pink or blue and white if you want to give this little curler cutie as a shower gift.

COLORFUL WALL COCK

Here we tell the tale of the cast-off cock.

You've seen these upholstery swatches often at your upholstery shop. This one measures 16 inches by 23 inches, and our good friend, the gentleman·who runs the upholstery shop, gave it to us just to see what we'd make out of it.

The background was bright mustard yellow, the colors across the bottom rang-

ing from reds through blues, greens, purples. We made our cock of felt scraps —brown head, turquoise tail, olive green body, raspberry legs and a bright red beak.

The border is bright green rickrack. The eye is a royal blue glass gem mosaic. The grommets were already in the top so all we had to do was slip three loops of plumber's chain through them, insert a brass curtain rod and we had a truly beautiful wall hanging.

POP TOP BOOT SCRAPER

When you recall the many tops to pop bottles you've thrown away in the past you'll wish you had saved some when you see what you can make with them.

All you need is a scrap of three-quarter-inch plywood. Ours is 15 inches by 12 inches.

Cover with pop tops, inside up, using inch nails so you can turn the plywood over when you finish nailing on the pop bottle tops and bend the nail ends down, thus securing them firmly.

Now you have a perfect doormat that acts as a boot scraper, and believe me, it is tough enough to take plenty of hard wear.

If you want to get fancy you can paint some of the pop tops one color, then paint others a contrasting color to spell out the word 'Hi!" or "Welcome" or your initials. But after a little mud gets on your artistry it may disappear. However, if you're giving this practical door mat as a gift you might want to dress it up. It is one of the most popular "some-things" we've ever created out of nothing so we want you to know who told us about it.

Contributed by
MARY MARGARET TOBIAS

SPECTACULAR EAGLE TRAY

This magnificent serving tray, which is 24 inches in circumference, was originally a grease can lid; and if you have a friend who runs a Gasoline Service Station perhaps you can coax him into saving you the lid from a grease drum so you can make a tray like this for your home.

This tray was sprayed in off white; then we pasted on the eagle, stars and date after cutting them from one of those hanging linen wall calendars.

We use the back for serving and the front for display, hanging the tray as a wall ornament when it isn't in use.

Our Eagle Tray is not only handsome, it's capacious and practical and everyone who sees it wants one like it.

Contributed by
CELIA HODENKAMP

TEA BAG SACHET

If you love Constant Comment Tea as much as we do you're sure to appreciate its heady scent of clove and orange as much as its nicely spiced taste. But did you know that you can make wonderful sachets from Constant Comment Tea Bags? Just place a tea bag in a piece of net and tie with a decorative velvet or satin bow. There's your sachet, all ready to tuck between linens or lingerie where it gives off a heavenly scent.

If you want to give these sachets to others as gifts you can dress up the outside a little more by adding sequins or tiny flowers or several small bows— get as fancy as you please. And if you want to give away several of these Constant Comment Sachets at one time, wrap them in a gift box of your own making. Just take any discarded cardboard box and line with foil to keep the scent nicely protected, then cover the outside with gift wrapping paper and add some bows or flowers. Now the outside of the gift is as lovely as the inside.

JINGLE BELL DOOR KNOCKER

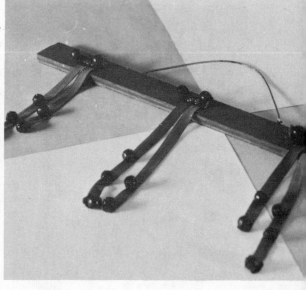

We don't remember where we got the little "Kiddy Halter" complete with jingling bells that inspired this guest announcer, but we do know that the bells were hanging from our fruit trees to keep the birds away for years when we suddenly realized we could make something from them.

So we cut them down, painted the webbing red and the bells black. Then we cut a board about 3 inches wide and 30 inches long and painted it red and nailed our bells to it with ornate brass upholstery tacks.

We looped a wire in two cup hooks at the top of the board, hung the bells outside our door and now guests jingle them to tell us they're about to descend on us.

Golden Coasters from Prune Jar Lids.
(See page 93.)

Felt Pen Painting on Pressed Wood.
(See page 75.)

Little Curler Cutie Doll.
(See page 62.)

Floating Angel of Mercy.
(See page 74.)

ers à Fresca.
page 70.)

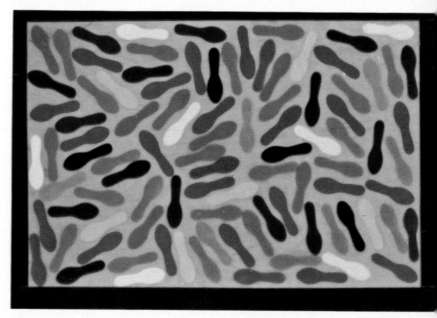

Ice Cream Spoon Pop Art Painting
(See page 28.)

Bleach or Detergent Bottle Bird Feed
(See page 83.)

BASKETBALL HOOP BECOMES FLORAL PHANTASY

When you set out to make something from nothing, you frequently find that the something you wind up with is not always the something you intended to make. Such was the case with the item pictured, which we can only describe as a "Floral Phantasy" since we haven't yet discovered a use for it. However it is much too beautiful to discard so we'll tell you how it "growed."

We intended to use this basketball hoop which our son had outgrown as the basis for a woven tapestry wall hanging, so we bound the rim in burlap and made seven spokes of burlap which we meant to use as our loom. As the beginning of our Aztec design we wound the rim of the hoop with bright coral velvet. Instantly it began to take on a character of its own and before we knew it instead of weaving a fabric wall tapestry we were twining garlands of flowers here and there and making the centers of green glass gem mosaics and when we finished we had this rather ethereal hoop of white flowers, coral velvet and green leaves that could be hung on a patio wall or in an entranceway, or it might even be suspended from the ceiling by a chain and made into a mock chandelier with paper lanterns depending from it. Some may say that this time we made a nothing from something, but we still love our beautiful Floral Phantasy and if you decide to make one let us know what you do with it.

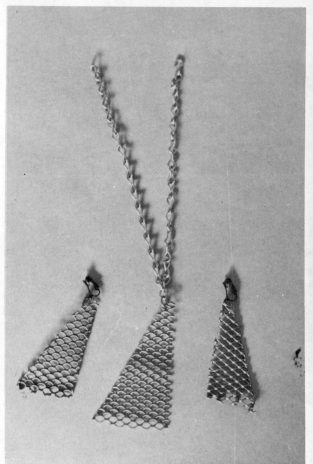

SWINGING JEWELRY SET

These swinging golden (?) earrings with matching pendant were cut from a piece of the grille wire used to cover radio speakers. Hooked onto a pair of ear clamps and a piece of plumber's chain they make a lightweight, handsome set of way out jewelry. To make sure the cut edges of the wire wouldn't hook into sweaters or hair we dropped a blob of gold sealing wax on each wire end, thereby adding to the handcrafted look of these "jools."

NEW LOOK FOR A FIREPLACE SCREEN

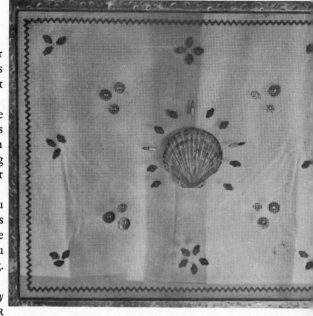

We hope you haven't thrown away your old rusty fireplace screen because here's one way you can reclaim it and put it to effective use during the summer.

Just spray paint it any color you like and add shells, shell macaroni, gem glass mosaics and old Christmas light bulbs in an airy, open design. Now you can hang this rejuvenated screen in your patio or den.

If you feel even more ambitious you can embroider flowers on it since it is possible to work the small mesh wire just as you would needlepoint. Now you have an even more elegant wall hanging.

Contributed by
WANITA DRAPER

SPONGE MINI-WHALE

Here's a fun way to amuse a youngster and also to see that he enjoys taking his daily bath. Cut a whale from a foam rubber bathtub sponge, stick a paper fastener in it for an eye and sail your whale in the bathtub. Tiny as he is he cuts a big splash with the chillen.

TIN CAN PAINTING

This simple but strikingly colorful wall plaque is perfect for a child's room or nursery. The background is black vinyl stretched over thin plywood inserted in a very old ornate frame painted fire engine red. The flowers and leaves are cut from tin cans and pasted to the black background.

SOME ORIGINAL CANDLEHOLDERS

Frequently we have only to look at an object to see at first glance that it can be used for a purpose totally removed from that for which it was made. Such was the case when we first met up with a hose connector—in this case the kind used to join plastic hose together. Immediately it suggested a candleholder. So all we did was paint the hose connector in two shades to emphasize its original design: French Blue on the bottom and violet on top. We inserted a gold tapered candle and had the loveliest candleholder imaginable. And, of course, you can use several at a time in a circle or in pairs.

We set the hose connector on top of an old funnel to dry and realized we had created an even more interesting candleholder. So we used the same two colors—French Blue on the funnel, and violet and blue on the hose connector—and now we can't say which candleholder we like best.

ROCK CARVINGS FOR GARDEN AND PATIO

Would you like to adorn your garden or your patio with all sorts of interesting Tiki types, escutcheons, plaques and other sculpture or statuary—at virtually no cost? Then do as an enterprising and imaginative neighbor of ours did and next time you visit a nursery supply store where they handle decorative rock, ask for some odd pieces of limestone without shell embedded in them.

The decorative pieces you see here were carved by an amateur without any artistic training or previous sculpturing experience. He just traces his design on the limestone piece with a sharply pointed awl and then starts chipping away. After bringing the design into relief he's ready to mold and polish to the desired degree of perfection.

This particular kind of limestone is soft and malleable and responsive to the creative touch, and you can have a whale of a lot of fun peopling your garden with these original creations and soon earn the reputation of being an accomplished sculptor.

Contributed and executed by
CECIL RANDLEMAN

PATCHWORK HASSOCK

The cushion of this shriekingly colorful hassock was made by covering an old pillow with brilliant yellow drapery fabric to which I baseball-stitched patches of upholstery samples in vivid shades of blue, green, purple and blue. The multi-colored fringe was made by knotting strands of blue, green, yellow and red yarn into a length of single crochet chain stitching. The cushion was then fastened to plywood which we bolted to the wrought iron legs from a former T.V. stand.

FLOWERS A FRESCA

"Well, let's see you make something from this!" is always a challenge we cannot resist. But when a friend brought us a Fresca six-pack carrier we secretly thought we were stumped. However, the same friend gave us a can of Pink Christmas Snow and, combining the two gifts, we came up with a "something" as beautiful as any we have ever made. Of course you must imagine its color scheme if you are to appreciate its remarkable beauty.

The Fresca container, covered with the entire can of Pink Christmas Snow acquired a delicate, ethereal air, for the pink snow, when it dries, gives the appearance of thick flocking.

The flowers are hand-made of red cellophane, pink, red and orange variegated Madras Tissue paper and the orange-pink wrappings from a package of Zee coral toilet tissue. Then we tucked white lace paper doilies around the flowers at the point where they emerge from the container, just to make them appear more delicate.

We made two discoveries in creating these flowers. One is the fact that flowers made from colored cellophane are breathtakingly beautiful because light shines through them, enhancing their loveliness. Also, you can make flowers of any size and of any material simply by following these simple instructions: Cut paper in squares, any desired size, accordion pleat and tie in center. Then pull the folds down to the center one by one. The result is a flamboyant, spectacular flower.

Contributed by
OPAL TREMAINE

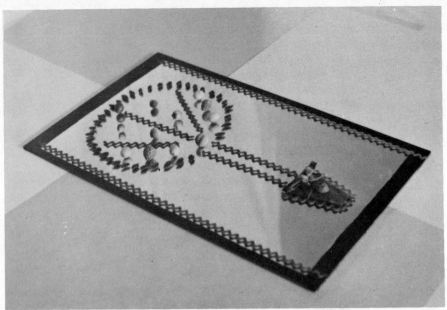

TREE BLOOMING MIRROR

Almost everyone has an old mirror around the house that has lost its frame and no longer gives back an honest reflection. This particular mirror had a band of black across the top so we added three more bands, then pasted on a tree of olive green rickrack, some artificial fruit in bright yellow and orange tones—tiny lemons, apples and oranges—and made a flower pot at the base of green felt. Now our little mirror hangs proudly in the entrance hall where everyone exclaims over its springlike beauty.

PATIO PEOPLE CALLER

This unusual dinner gong may not be loud enough to call them in from the North Forty, but it's guaranteed to wake Pop from his Sunday nap and tell him it's Chow Time.

You can make your own in just about five minutes. Just hang a pie pan in the center of an old tire rim and stick a screwdriver in the side of the rim for a gong. Paint your rim and pie pan in two tones—we did ours in black and fire engine red, adding a bold black spatter of paint in the center of the pie pan to suggest action. You might want to put your family brand on your pie pan.

THE GOODS AND THE BADS

We call this dramatic (and puzzling) feather painting "The Goods and the Bads" because it points a moral. It happened in this wise: We found an old wood scrap (pressed wood) with a division in the center and decided it would make a good background for a feather painting which we wanted to include in this book because statistics say 50 per cent of our population still live on farms so there must be quite a few chicken feathers around.

So we painted the top half black and edged it in white rickrack; then we painted the bottom half white and edged it in black rickrack. Since we have two strains of chickens on our ranch, White Wyandottes and Black Minorcas, we decided to make a white (or good) angel and a black (or bad) angel to show the choice we face in life.

The "bad" angel, bearing a strand of red beads, offers us a crown of jewels. (Beware! These are phony!)

But the "good" angel, bearing pearls, offers us a pink plush heart.

If you remember with nostalgia the old moralistic paintings our great grandmothers used to display, you too may want to make a story telling plaque like this one. And if you don't have your own chickens, despair not. Many craft stores carry packaged feathers in various colors. They call them "Grackle."

BREADBOX METAMORPHOSIS

"What can you make from an old bread-box?" our neighbor asked, in that challenging tone of voice that invariably fires our creative spark.

"Well, we could punch holes in the back and hang it up as a bathroom cabinet," we replied, "but it might be more fun to make it into a portable desk."

We were thinking of our daughter-in-law when we said this. She writes constantly to her husband who is in the Navy and she moves so often trying to keep up with him that her writing things are always on the go.

So we painted the breadbox turquoise and black and screwed a drawer handle to the top and pasted on four of those ornate steel ornaments that you find on office file dividers.

The evolving portable desk was painted black inside and we placed a foil doily in it to liven it up and to catch ink spills. Now it holds letters, writing paper, sealing wax, etc., etc., etc. and is ready to go anywhere.

FLOATING ANGEL OF MERCY

This cool drink dispenser floats at your side in the family pool and when you feel the need of additional refreshment you simply lower the angel to half mast.

The base is the top of a five-gallon paint can painted gold. In the center we placed the inner tube from a Suzuki cycle, anchoring it with Wilhold Glue. We stuck a candystriped plastic straw over the tube valve and hung a little red angel aloft on it.

Scoffers said it wouldn't float, but miraculously enough it does, though we still can't figure out why. Stripe the tire any two colors you like. We striped in white and orange interspersed with pieces of black tube showing through.

WISHBONE EARRINGS

Drill holes in the tops of two wishbones, gild them and wire on three multi-color beads then attach to ear bobs and you have a pair of dingling, dangling earrings in tune with the times.

Your biggest problem, as ours, may be to get the family to relinquish wishbones for such an aesthetic purpose. At any rate be sure to scrape the wishbones and let them dry thoroughly before turning them into earrings, or necklaces, which you can do simply by stringing them on bead wire, alternating with beads.

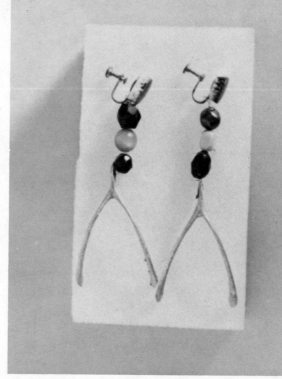

BEAUTIFIED BATH BOTTLE

This is an I. W. Harper bottle but any bottle may be glamorized simply by gilding and adding glass gem mosaics. Ours are amethyst and turquoise color.

The reclaimed bottle makes a pleasant ornament in bath or dressing room or it may be used for bath salts.

FELT PEN PAINTING ON PRESSED WOOD

Ken Vincent, the gentleman who runs our local cabinet shop is kind enough to give us his wood scraps. This one is 15½ inches by 25 inches and it was already painted white on one side so it required no sizing.

We had just bought some felt water color pens for a few cents a piece and we wanted to see what we could do with them so we used them to create our hen. She is shocking pink with purple comb and tail markings against a blue sky and lime colored grass and her eggs are white with red artificial flowers pasted on to simulate the measle markings.

CANDLEHOLDER AND DESK STAND

If your hobby is making something from nothing you learn not to throw things away but to take them apart and save the parts against that crucial moment of inspiration.

We took a string mop head apart and discovered that the part the mop head runs through makes a perfect candleholder. We painted it French Blue and pasted it to a wood scrap painted the same color, added a turquoise border and a few turquoise beads and used it as a holder for a gilded candle. The base makes a perfect desk stand on which you can rest pen or pencil if you wish.

PAPER BOX CURLER CADDY

No one would recognize this Honey Graham Cracker Box in its new guise as a Curler Caddy. We lined it with emerald green foil culled from an Azalea plant which was an Easter gift.

Then we covered the outside with variegated Madras Tissue Paper in rich shades of deep blue and violet. We painted the curlers royal blue and pasted them on top on either side of a royal blue satin ribbon left over from a former corsage. The front of the box is decorated with jade green earring buttons, three turquoise rubber bands and four light green toothpicks.

GLITTER FALL PAPER WEIGHT

This lovely glitter fall paperweight is made from a Gulden Mustard Jar turned upside down on a wood scrap painted black and edged with olive green rickrack. Glue the jar to the stand and add a gilded cookie press cutter and a few green glass gem mosaics to the top. Inside you put the heads of some artificial flowers, one or two leaves (all plastic of course) and fill with water and a teaspoon full of gold glitter. We gilded the cap of the jar and pasted olive green rickrack to it.

Any time you invert this attractive paperweight it spills a shower of gold glitter through the flowers in the manner of those old fashioned snow fall paperweights. You can make them with any shape jar that will cap securely.

Contributed by
FRANCES BREWER

ENGLISH SPUR DOOR KNOCKER

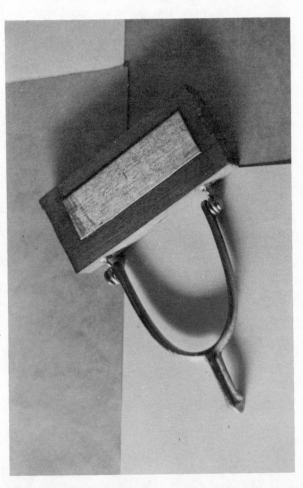

One of the most beautiful somethings that we have ever managed to contrive from a nothing is this elegant door knocker and it took exactly five minutes to make.

We simply screwed two brass cup hooks into a walnut-stained wood scrap 5½ inches by 2½ inches by 1 inch and hung a gilded English riding spur on the hooks, then closed them.

We pasted a piece of thin brass foil to the wood and the door knocker was complete. The owner's name may be painted on the foil with Pactra Enamel or it may be etched into the metal.

ROMANTIC ALUMINUM AMULET

Though you search the wide world over we doubt you'll ever find another necklace like this one. The amulet is made from a piece of aluminum—all that was left of our neighbor's aluminum ladder after a brush fire that raged through our ranches several years ago.

What makes the amulet romantic and of special interest is the fact that our neighbor happened to be Ronald Reagan, now Governor of California.

GLORIFIED CLAM SHELL

Just another clamshell, you would have said, had you seen this shell lying on the beach at Malibu as we did one summer morning. But gilded and covered with gem mosaics the color of amethysts, jasper, carnelian and topaz, adorned with Christmas Bulbs for antennae, and nailed to a walnut stained plaque with ornate brass upholstery tacks that also make up the border, our clam shell became a fabulous butterfly that now adorns the wall of our den.

MOCK EMBROIDERY WALL PANEL

We appreciate and admire true embroidery, but since we are an oaf with a needle, we prefer to paste rather than sew. That is how we came to make this mock embroidery panel which may be used as a wall ornament.

We covered a wood scrap 11 inches by 11 inches with rich coral velvet, added two strips of bright green rickrack at the base and pasted on a yarn flower with coiled yarn flowerets of turquoise and royal blue. The flowers are the heads from discarded plastic lilies of the valley, each encircled with a tiny brass ring of the kind used in jewelry making.

The overall effect is colorful and impressive but it takes less than one tenth the time it would take to execute the plaque in hand stitching.

EVOLUTION OF A FRUIT CAKE TIN

When a good friend gave us a fruit cake for Christmas in a handsome foil container marbled in silver, green and turquoise we naturally saved the container, sensing it would some day make a "something."

And sure enough, long after Christmas, that beautiful silver, blue and green foil container became this handsome Maltese Cross. We decorated it with glass gem mosaics in royal blue, emerald green and topaz and pasted it on a square of olive green felt, pasted that to a square of black rippled cardboard, once backing for an upholstery swatch, and added dark green and olive green rickrack borders. The center border is made from those little black Nuace corners that you use to hold snapshots in photography albums. They make beautiful borders for many things and come in various colors as well as black.

We thought the preponderance of essentially sombre tones here would result in a dreary effect, but actually quite the opposite is true. The cross is strikingly beautiful against its low key surroundings.

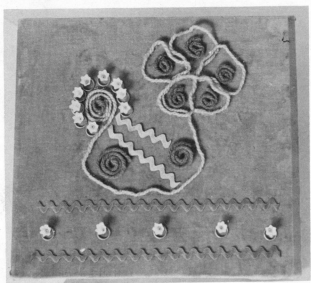

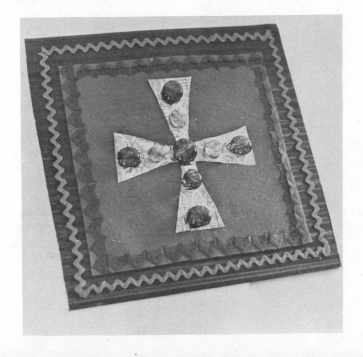

HORSE PLAQUE ON BURLAP

The background of this nursery plaque is a wood scrap 13 inches by 10½ inches covered with burlap. To this we pasted a square of raspberry construction paper and on the construction paper we mounted a black plastic mold of the type used by children for clay modeling, in the shape of a horsehead in bas relief. The blaze down the front of the horse's face is uncooked white rice. His mane is made from oatmeal and above the oatmeal we scattered crumbled dry sage. We added a few plastic red flowers in the mane and at the bottom and now have a handsome birthday gift for a youngster.

Suggestion contributed by
CELIA HODENKAMP

BERRY BOX BIRD CAGE

"Isn't it a shame to throw out those cute little plastic green boxes berries come in!" a friend once exclaimed and of course the remark was made to the wrong person because I never throw anything out.

"Don't ever throw them away, you can make lovely bird cages out of them or hanging planters," I told my friend, and proceeded to make this little cage in five minutes to demonstrate the point.

We just put some Easter basket grass (shredded green waxed paper) in the bottom and added two pink eggs (the ends of two ladies shoe trees). Then we hung a little paper bird from the top basket, wired the two baskets together with artificial lilac flowerets and hung a little silver chain from the top so the basket can be hung in a child's room.

What a perfect little Easter gift for the youngsters to give each other at Bunny Time.

Contributed by
LILLIAN GREER

EGG POACHER PORTRAIT FRAME

This portrait frame is so lush looking people refuse to believe that it is made from that portion of an egg poacher in which the egg cups usually rest.

We gilded it, bordered it in rich chocolate brown Pactra enamel and outlined each circular opening with the same shade of brown, then pasted on some topaz glass gem mosaics.

We attached a little chain so that the portrait holder may be hung up and we also pasted a tin foil pie pan (gilded) to the back so that you can stand it up if decide not to hang it.

CHURCH STEEPLE NURSERY PLAQUE

Originally this wooden plaque had the hands of a clock attached to it and was used as an "out-to-lunch" sign.

We took off the hands, pasted on a scrap of chintz in a church steeple pattern; added a border of bright green plastic tape and behold—a nursery plaque.

Contributed by
CELIA HODENKAMP

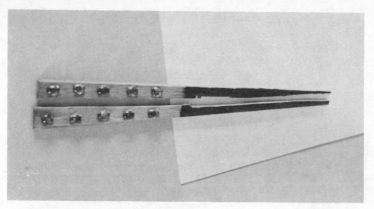

CHOP STICK CHIGNON PINS

Accidents are the mother of discoveries. Some of our most remarkable "some-things" evolve from mistakes. A case in point is these chop sticks which happened when we attempted to split a window shade lath and it cracked unevenly.

Reversing the ends we discovered we had a pair of perfect chop sticks. So we painted the tops soft jade green, the bottoms deep blue green and pasted soft blue cabachons lifted from a broken necklace in a pattern along the top of each stick.

The resulting chop sticks are so lovely they may be worn as chignon pins.

COAT HANGER BUTTERFLY

Join two coat hangers by twisting the handles together, cover with kitchen foil and paste on glass mosaics to make a patio butterfly. Edges are taped with plastic tape. "Feelers" are made from old Christmas Tree lights. The butterfly may be attached to spike or painted broom handle and driven into the ground to give the appearance of being in flight.

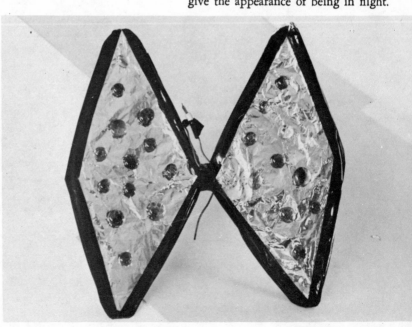

TAPPING THE LIGHT FANTASTIC

If you're lucky enough to find a shoe
stretcher of the type shown decorate it
as we did and hang it on your bathroom
or bedroom door as a door knocker. We
painted ours black with a brilliant yellow
shoe; added turquoise rickrack, green
glass gem mosaics and a boutonniere of
posies in wild shades of orange, yellow
and pink.

Now friends are begging for door
knockers like ours but you can't always
find these old fashioned shoe stretchers
so if you find one, grab it!

BLEACH OR DETERGENT BOTTLE
BIRD FEEDER

We cut the center out of a gallon-size Cold
Water All Detergent Bottle to make this
glamorous bird feeder but you can use
any plastic bleach or detergent bottle if
you wish. To decorate, use whatever
comes to hand. We used plastic grapes
and silver grape leaves because the bottle
is a bright blue. We wired the decorations on, hung the feeder from a tree,
sprinkled bird seed and bread crumbs in
the bottom and now we hear all sorts of
pleasant thank-you songs every day.

Contributed by
WANITA DRAPER

GLAMOROUS RECEPTACLE FOR OLD RAZOR BLADES

What to do with old razor blades? Well we frequently use them as design borders around paintings. We just gild them or paint them and paste them on. They have a lot of artistic interest. But if you just want to get rid of them aesthetically do as we did and take an old cardboard box, in this case bright gold; but you could gild yours, paint a red square in the front and paint your razor blades black and paste blades around the opening at the top and across the red patch on the front.

Now you have a safe way of getting rid of blades and an attractive ornament for your bathroom.

SOAP STILL LIFE

A friend of ours brought us from Vienna some beautifully colored soap in the shape of fruit; and it was too lovely to use so we made it into this still life. We just pasted an oval of lime green felt to a japanned serving tray 12 by 10 inches in diameter, then pasted the soap to it and added a few baby pine cones and a border of olive green rickrack. The plaque may be hung in the breakfast room where we guarantee it will bring admiring comments.

PINK ELEPHANT NURSERY PLAQUE

Here's another treatment for a discarded fireplace screen.

Paste on elephants cut from a pink nylon pile rug scrap; add felt flowers in magenta, turquoise, lime. Sprinkle on sequins and pearls and you have a nursery plaque that anyone would welcome at a baby shower.

PLASTIC STRAW MOBILE

To make this ethereal, eye-catching mobile, simply tie four strands of nylon fish line to an old calendar holder. Weight the ends—we used brass lamp parts. Then wire bunches of pink, blue and green plastic straws together at the middle and anchor them to the fish line.

Hung in a window where the sunlight can glance off the shimmering plastic straws, this mobile adds a bright spot of color to any room.

PETIT BIKINI BEACH BAG

We have our friend who runs the upholstery shop to thank for this chic little tote bag. He gave us the scrap of soft blue and gold upholstery fabric from which to make it—it measured about 27 inches by 13 inches.

We lined it with a piece of a white bathroom towel, hemmed the top and bottom and put grommets in the top, then buttonhole stitched the sides with grey-blue yarn. We knotted white cording through the grommets and now if we were brave enough we'd put a Bikini in it.

In any case it makes a beautiful beach bag.

And, by the way, if you don't have grommets, make a draw string or use eyelets and smaller cording.

Contributed by
MARGIE MOSS

Supplies by
GEORGE MOCKRY'S
UPHOLSTILLERY

STAINED GLASS WINDOW

We have said and we repeat that some of our loveliest effects have been created by accident. Here is a perfect example.

A friend brought us this styrofoam packing fragment and we thought it would look well gilded so we sprayed it with gold paint. We made the mistake of using lacquer base spray paint instead of the new plastic spray paints made especially for styrofoam and as a result the fibers were pulled together revealing strands of blue within the styrofoam. By accident we held our styrofoam piece up to the light to examine it more thoroughly and as the sunlight streamed through the gold and blue background we discovered we had a perfect stained-glass window. We crumpled a piece of pale blue plastic laundry bag and stuffed it in the center and as the sunlight sifted through it we now had a Hope Diamond in our window. Everyone who sees this lovely creation agrees it is breathtakingly beautiful. Of course to enjoy its beauty it must be hung against a window where the sun will strike it.

RUG SCRAP PICTURE FRAME

Picture frames run so high today many people forego the pleasure of having a painting simply because they can't afford the cost of the frame. After we covered this 19 by 36 inch plywood with burlap and pasted on flowers in red, yellow, green and blue made of fabric scraps, we added centers of bright blue glass gem mosaics, stems of green rickrack and green plastic straws, then wondered how we could fashion a frame.

A week earlier a friend drove up to see us in a pick-up truck with a few scraps of deep pile nylon carpeting in the back of rich blue and green. He asked us if we could use the scraps for anything and we said we probably could. Now they came to mind. Cut and tacked to our plywood they made a perfect frame, interesting in texture and just the right color to complement the painting.

SKIM BOARD COFFEE TABLE

Has junior outgrown his skim board? If he has and you coax it away from him you have the beginnings of a most unusual coffee table. Now all you need to do is fasten the skim board to the wrought iron base of a portable television stand and your coffee table is ready for decoration.

We painted the top of ours off white and decorated it with botanical prints, outlined the prints in bright swirls of orange and green, and continued the green and orange swirls around the edge as a border; and now all we had left to do was apply a coat of varnish as protection from spills and stains.

Contributed by
CELIA HODENKAMP

We made a gigantic boo-boo when we tried to make a gargantuan wall hanging out of this one-time coffee table top measuring 24 inches by 36 inches. The mistake was not in the concept, which proved sound, but in the execution. A friend gave us a whole box full of ground up automobile windshield glass—one of those challenge gifts—let's see you make something out of this, we dare you! Well, ground-up windshield glass is bright and sparkly and suggested snow and we painted the coffee table top a soft blue-grey, intending to draw a stark black tree in outline against this sere ground and pile windshield glass sparkle along its tortured limbs. We soon learned that our color scheme was depressing and quite unimpressive so we began brightening things up.

When we finished we had the most blatantly beautiful bo tree you could imagine and our color scheme instead of being bleak had become positively lusty. Now the background is lemon yellow bordered in brick red and avocado green and the gem glass mosaics and cut out felt flowers and butterfly are earth-shaking hues of magenta, red, purple, turquoise, royal blue and shocking pink.

We didn't give up and we're glad that we didn't, because now our bo tree brightens up an entire room and earns constant admiring exclamations from those who behold it.

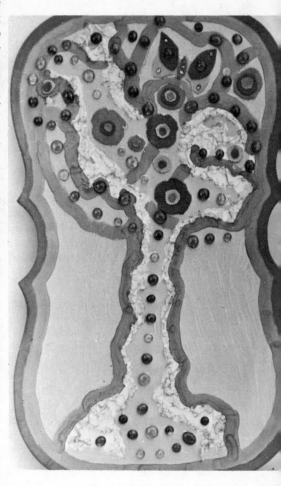

PERKY PATCHWORK PONY PLAQUE

What can you do with an old bamboo match stick curtain 24 inches by 22 inches that has lost its mate as well as its verve?

Here's what we did. We gilded it and pasted on upholstery squares in soft tapestry patterns of red, blue, green, turquoise, yellow and violet. We added a royal blue glass gem mosaic for an eye. The halter, rein, saddle, hoofs and tail are of black patent leather, also studded with mosaics.

Now we have a pert and perky pony plaque adored by every young horse lover.

WHEN KNIGHTHOOD WAS IN FLOUR

What does the kitchen have to offer in the way of aesthetic possibilities? We've only scratched the surface—the possibilities are endless, but we consider this a fair beginning.

Someone dared us to make something from leftover egg shells and dried coffee grounds and since we never pass up a challenge we decided to try.

Here's what developed: We took a piece of wood scrap 24 inches by 24 inches and covered the entire surface with our own homemade glue which we made with liquid ironing starch and flour. (Just add enough flour to the starch to make it the consistency you like. If you want to keep it over a long period add a few drops of Oil of Wintergreen as a preservative. You can get it from any druggist. Or store in the refrigerator.)

Next we sprinkled on egg shells in the shape of a horse, added a knight made of beads and gave him a pipe cleaner for a lance and a gold button for a shield. For a border we pasted on cut-up containers from packages of Mother's Chocolate Mint Cookies. We sprayed the whole

thing with gold paint and painted the horse with Pactra French Blue enamel. The knight turquoise, boot and head shocking pink.

The metamorphosis was complete. We finished with an impressive and beautiful wall hanging that looks as if it is framed in great chunky solid gold nuggets!

HUFF, THE SCRAPPY DRAGON

Huff is one of the most beloved somethings we've ever made from nothing and so colorful that he can only be referred to as a character.

To make him we used scrap yarn about 4 inches long of every conceivable color and pulled it through a piece of burlap 4 inches wide by 36 inches long, just as if we were working a looped rug, then cut the loops. We stitched the burlap to a folded piece of upholstery fabric of very thick, sturdy texture, also 36 inches long, but about 6 inches wide.

The head is a huge scarlet pompom 6 inches in circumference. The eyes are spools painted black with black buttons glued to the ends. Huff's crown is made from red artificial flowers. His ears are old Christmas Tree bulbs painted green. His tongue is a scrap of fire-red flannel snitched from the seat of my pajamas and his collar is bright orange satin ribbon fastened with a rhinestone shoe buckle.

Every youngster who sees Huff wants him for her own so if you make one you'll have to make several and you'd better start saving yarn scraps right now.

HURRICANE CANDLE HOLDER

We found a dust-covered abandoned chimney from one of our ranch lanterns lying forsaken and forlorn in our garage and after polishing it to glistening cleanliness and pasting it to a discarded wooden dish we set about making a glamorous hurricane patio candle holder out of it.

The color scheme is purple, green and silver, carried out by ringing the top of the glass chimney with purple glass beads and painting purple, green and silver squiggles on the glass itself.

We decked the base with encircling green Christmas tree beads plus an outer circle of huge green glass gem mosaics and now we have an ultra-gorgeous patio accessory, rescued from the limbo of forgotten nothings.

STRAWS ON STRAW

A straw place mat purchased at the Salvation Army Store for five cents provides the background for this really lovely wall hanging. We discovered that if you cut plastic straws (in this case pink, green and blue) in various lengths you can embroider them to fabrics or straw and make beautiful, colorful, irridescent designs of truly unusual beauty.

We kept our pattern very simple, allowing the straws themselves to dictate the design but you can become as sophisticated as you wish in your straw embroidery, cutting the straws to various lengths and making exciting parquet effects if you have the time and inclination to do so. You can also do this straw embroidery on beach bags and on matchstick bamboo.

The frame, which contributes to the overall excitement of the completed hanging, evolved by accident. We intended to make the border of straws but after pasting them in place with Wilhold Glue found we had too much of a muchness. We stripped off the border straws but the glue ridges remained. Now we had a textured frame. And we had not only discovered a new craft of straw embroidery but a new inexpensive way to make all sorts of thrilling patterned and textured frames simply by dripping Wilhold Glue on them, letting it dry, then painting over the dried glue. Here we

painted with Prussian Blue, Veridian Green and Raw Umber oils, then rubbed on streaks of gold paint. You can make your own Gesso Frames by this method.

Creative spark supplied by
MARGIE MOSS

BREAD WRAPPINGS BLOOM IN BEAUTY

Yes, the exquisite golden flowers you see grouped so gracefully in a champagne bottle were made from the cellophane inner wrappings of Sheep Herder Whole Grain Bread.

Just fold the wrappings in half, using three to a flower, cut the edges to eliminate folds; then accordion pleat, tie in center and pull each fold down from the top to the bottom, working from the outside folds inward.

Fasten the flowers to balloon stems painted green (or wrapped in florist's tape); or fasten them to the stems from old artificial flowers.

To give an air of elegance to our champagne bottle we added a diplomat's ribbon of lime green grosgrain ribbon fastened with a topaz gem culled from an old house slipper.

CHUCKLE BONE NECKLACE

Believe it or not the gleaming, glorious "pearl" that forms the focal point of this necklace was sliced from a knucklebone of beef. We saw it floating in the soup and instantly glimpsed its beauty potential.

Fishing it out we found it needed nothing more than drying off to become a thing of beauty, for it has a natural pearlized gleaming irridescence of its own. We pasted it to the top of an insurance man's calendar pad, surrounded it with pearls, colorful beads, and anchored the whole with great glistening globs of pink and blue irridescent sealing wax, and we defy anyone to guess its origin. When the knee bone's connected to the "knobules" you have a necklace that really pops eyes!

FAMILY PORTRAIT HOLDER

Save the tops from Constant Comment Tea Containers (and the bottoms) or the tops and bottoms from cocoa cans, gild them and paste family snapshots in them (or on them) and make yourself a distinquished family portrait holder.

To make ours we cut a strip of shocking pink nylon pile rug 3½ inches wide and 24 inches long and pasted black lace down the center. To this background we glued our snapshots and hung our portrait holder by a black curtain ring.

Teenagers can make a whole series of hangings in different colors and cover an entire wall of their bedroom with these really attractive portrait holders.

Contributed by
JUNE PETERSEN

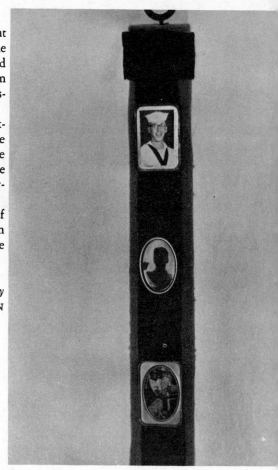

GOLDEN CHALICE BOUDOIR FLOWER HOLDERS

What can you make from two plastic cups used as airplane directional signals when a friend who works in a plastic parts plant brings them to you and says: "Let's see you turn these into something!"

It was tempting to consider the chalice-like plastic cups as candle chimneys, but since they were plastic we thought they might melt so we resisted that possibility.

We pasted them to two old candle holder bases, gilded them and now they had such a Holy Grail look we knew we had to turn them into something delicate and feminine. So we added glamorous encrustations of glass gem mosaics with sealing wax dribbled over them in bright shades of red and turquoise and added bouquets of violets and rock roses (artificial of course) and now our Golden Chalices are beautiful enough to grace any dressing table.

Creative spark supplied by
BELLE ALMARR

A VERY "SOLE-FUL" CANDY DISH

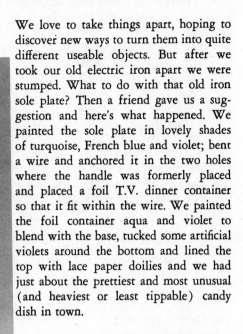

We love to take things apart, hoping to discover new ways to turn them into quite different useable objects. But after we took our old electric iron apart we were stumped. What to do with that old iron sole plate? Then a friend gave us a suggestion and here's what happened. We painted the sole plate in lovely shades of turquoise, French blue and violet; bent a wire and anchored it in the two holes where the handle was formerly placed and placed a foil T.V. dinner container so that it fit within the wire. We painted the foil container aqua and violet to blend with the base, tucked some artificial violets around the bottom and lined the top with lace paper doilies and we had just about the prettiest and most unusual (and heaviest or least tippable) candy dish in town.

Creative spark supplied by
MARY MARGARET TOBIAS

GOLDEN COASTERS FROM PRUNE JAR LIDS

Here's a slick way to get the family to eat more stewed prunes. Tell them you want the lids from the jars for coasters. We used lids from Del Monte Stewed Prunes for these coasters. We spray painted them with gold acrylic paint and pasted on impressive looking heraldic crests cut from an issue of *Holiday* Magazine.

We varnished the coasters to make them waterproof, added a bit of felt to the bottom to protect furniture and now guests exclaim in delight over our customized coasters.

Contributed by
CELIA HODENKAMP

DRESSED-UP SALAD DRESSING
BOTTLES

We love Girard Salad Dressing and we love the bottles it comes in. These two gleaming golden candleholders were made by gilding two Girard Salad Dressing bottles and pasting on hot pink and orange designs cut from a paper bag from a women's specialty shop. We gilded the candles to match the bases and we intend to create a whole assemblage of dressed-up salad dressing bottles to ornament our patio wall.

SWINGER RINGER

One of our young and lovely a-go-go neighbors asked us if we'd make a "Swinger Ringer" for her to hang outside the door next time she gave a party. Here's what we came up with: We took a plywood heart a friend had given us as a Christmas greeting, painted it black, trimmed it in green and turquoise and added three felt polka-dots, one black, one green, one blue. We made a bell from a tin can which we gilded and painted with a green, blue and turquoise design and hung a clapper inside it consisting of a twisted roll of tin cut from another tin can. We fastened a ringer to this bell clapper made from a black crystal chandelier drop.

The bell was fastened to the heart by means of a gold hair bandeau that provided just the right amount of "bounce" for the bell to jiggle and just the right amount of elegance, being gold.

Then as the crowning touch we hung a little plaque below the heart reading: "If you don't swing, don't ring!" Our Swinger Ringer was acclaimed a huge success.

Creative spark supplied by
MARY MARGARET TOBIAS

NO-STRAIN DESK ACCESSORY

We confess that we looked at this discarded dish strainer hundreds of times before we suddenly realized that it would make a good-looking, practical desk file.

All we did was paste a piece of plastic to the back and a grooved strip of molding in the first partition and spray the whole thing with—you guessed it—New Finish Acrylic Gold Spray Paint. (Of course you could paint your strainer black if you want it to look more masculine.)

To spark it up we added a shocking pink trim.

Now it holds letters, bills, photos, file cards, pads and writing paper, pens and pencils and keeps everything neat and easy to find.

Perfect gift for a studious teenager.

OLD JEWELRY INTO NEW

All of the jewelry you see here was made by forming new combinations from old jewelry or other bits and pieces. The pendant and earring drops were once charms on a charm bracelet. In a new combination they made a beautiful three-piece pendant and earring set.

The drop earrings were made from old coat buttons.

The hoop earrings, once drab white plastic, were sparkled with color by striping them violet, orange and turquoise.

The sunburst pendant was a pin that lost its clasp.

Take it from there and the sky is the limit when it comes to making new jewelry from old.

MAKE YOUR VERY OWN SOAP SAVER

Don't you hate to throw out all those little soap slivers just because they get too slippery to handle?

Well now you can save them and use them down to the last smallest smidgeon. Just cut a slit in a foam rubber sponge and slip the slippery slivers within. Now you can use your soap saver at the kitchen sink for hand washing; and if you make a spare, the young-uns can use that one in the bathroom.

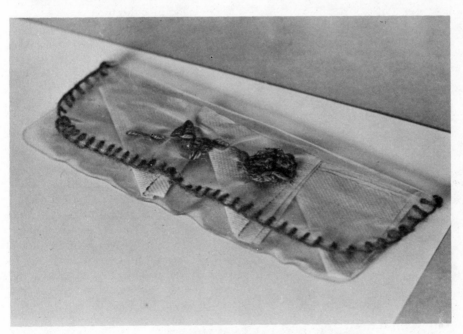

HANDSOME HANKY HOLDER

Slippers came in this plastic envelope 5½ inches wide by 13¾ inches long. We decided it would make a nice hanky holder or stocking kit so we simply made a red border of buttonhole stitching and added a bright red and green yarn flower and now we have a neat little storage case.

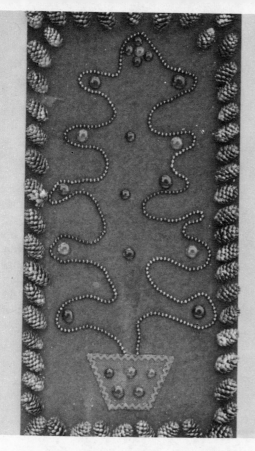

MASONITE DOOR ORNAMENT

Made from a scrap of brown masonite (unpainted), 15 inches by 32 inches, with the rough side out, this modernistic door plaque, which was originally intended as a Christmas ornament, proved handsome enough to leave out all year round.

To make it we pasted baby pine cones in a border around the edge and sprinkled them with gold glitter after brushing them with glue. Then we pasted dark green Christmas beads in the center in the shape of a Christmas Tree and added Christmas decorations to the tree of oliver green, topaz and emerald green glass gem mosaics.

The base is olive green felt trimmed in emerald green rickrack and green glass mosaics.

The masonite is weatherproof which makes it ideal for this use.

Contributed by
LILLIAN GREER

OUTDOOR BOOT SCRAPER

Want the kids to leave the mud behind them when they traipse indoors?

Just sink an old spade or shovel in concrete near the back door and they can use the handle to steady themselves while they scrape off the mud.

This is by no means a new suggestion since farm folks have been turning shovels into boot scrapers since time began. But in case you have an old shovel lying around you may want to put it back in service this way. We painted ours rust resistant silver and trimmed it in red and black. You can let the kids choose their own color scheme.

Did you ever have a "sore spot" to cover up on a wall and you didn't want to paint or repaper the whole wall? Here's a sneaky way to solve the problem that will win all sorts of praise from admiring onlookers.

Take four sheets of variegated Madras Tissue—we chose the hot pink and red color combination—and accordion pleat each sheet. Spread them out on a table so you can paste the sheets together to form a circle and tie a gilded pompon to the center.

* To keep the folds from falling toward the bottom when you hang this brashly beautiful wallflower, cut straws (pink plastic ones) in inch lengths and sew them between each fold, then hang your flower. We used a loop of folded red construction paper as a hanger, sewing it to the center of the flower in back and pasting it in place to be sure it would hold.

---

* Life-saving suggestion contributed by Margie Moss.

CASE OF THE CAMERA PURSE

The beautiful shimmering golden over the shoulder purse you see here was once the case of a camera: brown, ugly, discarded. We painted it turquoise inside with Pactra enamel and sprayed it gold outside and added some colorful felt cutouts and a plumber's chain for a handle. The centers of the flowers are lime and amethyst gem glass mosaics.

Now any little girl would be glad to wear this swinging purse or use it to house her mad money.

FROU FROU JEWEL BOX

This bedazzled and bedazzling jewel box started its career as a plain plastic box that once housed a hair brush. We gilded the box and then decorated it with white Whip-Wax, a fabulous product you will find at your nearest hobby supply shop. (Or write to the American Wax Company, Azusa, California for its location nearest you.) Whip-Wax, poured in a bowl and beaten up with water—using an ordinary egg beater—becomes a snow-white pliable plastic substance that you can put in a pastry toot and squeeze out in decorative forms. You can use it to decorate boxes, frames, candles; its uses are limitless. We sprinkled the Whip-Wax with Red Hots and now we have a unique jewel case.

MILLION DOLLAR MIRROR FROM THE DIME STORE

We made this simple little dime store mirror into a lovely boutique item by taking off the original metal frame and adding our own frame of Whip-Wax, that wonderful pliant, plastic that you beat up with water and put in a pastry toot to make all sorts of wonderful and exciting things. Here we tinted some Whip-Wax pink and squeezed it on the mirror in a border. When it dried we antiqued the pink by streaking it with gold paint on a dry brush. Then we squeezed white Whip-Wax over the pink and gold base in thick white squiggles. A teenager claimed the mirror immediately for her boudoir.

ISLAND PRINCESS BOOKEND

This graceful and enchanting Island Princess Bookend is not what she seems to be for she is of mysterious origin. Though she appears to be carved of gleaming, lustrous walnut she was actually made in a candle mold and set out to be a candle. And, in fact, if you were to insert a wick in the wax, she could be used as a candle. This candle mold and many others, equally lovely, may be obtained from the General Supplies Corporation in Fallbrook, California, along with instructions for pouring and together with all the materials you need to achieve results like this delightful figurine you see pictured. What a wonderful way to add interest to a mantle or den at minimum expense! You literally make something from nothing when candles turn into bookends and exquisite objects of art.

TAKE YOUR PICK—YOU CAN WORK WONDERS

'Twas only a grubby pick head. But we cast a magnificent foot-high candle in a metal pillar candle mold which we obtained from General Supplies Corporation in Fallbrook, California, and that's when the fun began. We gilded the candle and *turned it upside down,* securing it in the pick head with glue. We adorned the candle and base with wax flowers made from beeswax also obtained from General Supplies, and you must admit the end result is far from grubby—but what a stimulating coversation piece!

A Word in Parting

We hope you've enjoyed reading this book at least half as much as we enjoyed making the "somethings" you see in it.

You've probably discovered by now that this isn't a craft book or a book of instruction, it is simply a collection of ideas intended to encourage your ideas and so lead you on to a totally new kind of creative experience.

We've avoided details in favor of simplicity. And we never told you specifically how to make anything because we want you to do things your own way. You may find a simpler better way than we found; or at least it may seem simpler and better to you. In that case, do it your way. You may use different materials and different methods from those we employed and you may wind up with completely different results. All well and good.

Making nothings into somethings is a highly inventive sport but because it is inventive and spontaneous and original it releases tensions, unties knots of frustration, gives you a wonderful sense of pleasure and accomplishment.

So experiment, dare, improvise—enjoy every minute—and maybe you'll discover, as we did, that once you start making something from nothing, you find you can't stop, and, what's more, you don't want to stop!

List of Supplies and Suppliers

American Handicrafts, 1001 Foch Street, Fort Worth, Texas 76107

Bersteds Hobby Craft, Inc., Monmouth, Illinois 61462

General Supplies Company, Fallbrook, California 92028

American Wax Corporation, Azusa, California 91702

Home-Sew Incorporated, 1825 West Market St., Bethlehem, Penna. 18018

Ideas Unlimited, Graff Pub. Inc., 910 N. Marshfield, Chicago, Illinois 60612

Pack-O-Fun Scrap Craft Magazine, 1 Main St., Park Ridge, Ill. 60068

The Handcrafters, Waupun, Wisconsin 53963

Celluclay Instant Papier Mâché, Marshall, Texas 75670

AND YOUR LOCAL CRAFT OR HOBBY SUPPLY SHOP.